JOHN THOMPSON'S MODERN COURSE FOR THE PIANO

TEACHING LITTLE FINGERS TO PLAY ENSEMBLE

FOREWORD

THE Melodies contained in any Beginners' Book are necessarily very simple; hence, few harmonies are used. The addition of accompaniments, *to be played by the teacher or parent*, will add immeasurably to the musical interest of the tiny tunes and will make them sound quite "grown-up." The advantage is obvious.

ENSEMBLE PLAYING

The value of ensemble playing needs no comment and really cannot be started too soon. By means of ensemble playing the teacher or parent is enabled to *control tempo and rhythm* and to *encourage tonal nuance* from the very beginning. The child, too, having heard the accompaniments, carries the harmonies in his mind during his solitary practice periods with salutary results. In short, the elementary examples become "alive" for him immediately and sound like fragments of larger and more complex compositions.

In the Studio or in Pupils' Recitals, the Second Parts may be played by slightly more advanced students.

PRIMO AND SECONDO

Note that in the One Piano, Four-Hands arrangements, the pupil's part is sometimes *Primo* and sometimes *Secondo*.

This procedure is planned to develop the child as soloist and accompanist; with better musicianship as the objective.

It need hardly be pointed out that anything which promotes *listening* on the part of the pupil is invaluable and is so recognized by outstanding and successful music teachers. There is no single thing better adapted to develop this desired end than ensemble playing.

John Thompson

WILLIS MUSIC

EXCLUSIVELY DISTRIBUTED BY

HAL•LEONARD®
CORPORATION
7777 W. BLUEMOUND RD. P.O. BOX 13819
MILWAUKEE, WISCONSIN 53213

Birthday Party *(Page 8)

Piano-Four Hands

SECONDO

Birthday Party

Two-Pianos, Four Hands

PIANO II

*Refers to corresponding page in "Teaching Little Fingers to Play"

Sandman's Near (Page 9)

Piano-Four Hands

SECONDO

Sandman's Near

Two-Pianos, Four Hands

PIANO II

Base-ball Days (Page 10)

Piano-Four Hands

Base-ball Days

Two-Pianos, Four Hands

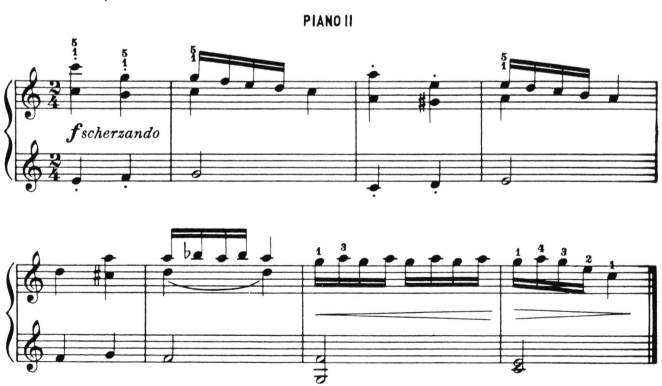

The Postman (Page 11)

Piano-Four Hands

PRIMO

The Postman

Two-Pianos, Four Hands

PIANO II

Rain on the Roof (Page 12)

Piano-Four Hands

PRIMO

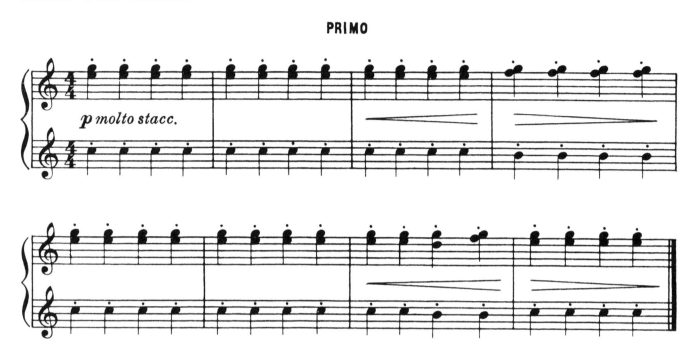

Rain on the Roof

Two-Pianos, Four Hands

PIANO II

Song of the Volga Boatmen (Page 13)

Piano-Four Hands

SECONDO

Song of the Volga Boatmen

Two-Pianos, Four Hands

PIANO II

A Message (Page 14)

Piano-Four Hands

SECONDO

A Message

Two-Pianos, Four Hands

PIANO II

Chimes (Page 15)

Piano-Four Hands

PRIMO

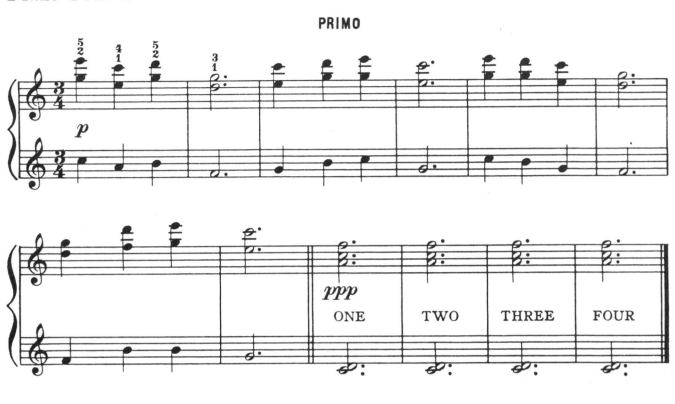

Chimes

Two-Pianos, Four Hands

PIANO II

Good King Wenceslas <small>(Page 16)</small>

Piano-Four Hands

SECONDO

Good King Wenceslas

Two-Pianos, Four Hands

PIANO II

Lazy Mary (Page 17)

Piano-Four Hands

SECONDO

Lazy Mary

Two-Pianos, Four Hands

PIANO II

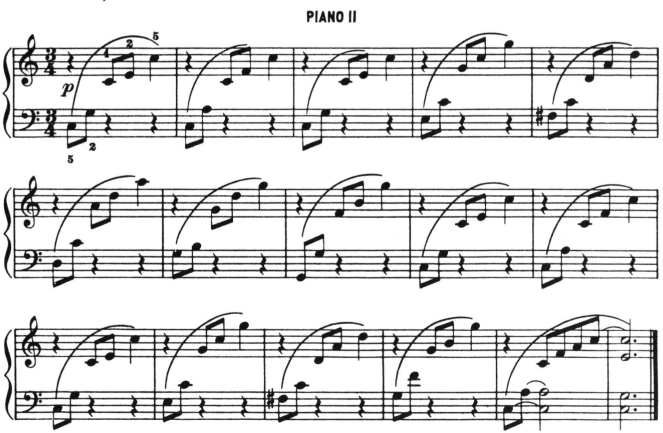

Betty and Bill (Page 18)

Piano-Four Hands

SECONDO

Betty and Bill

Two-Pianos, Four Hands

PIANO II

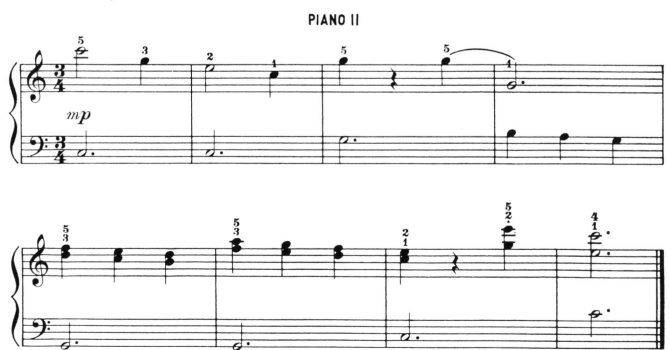

Flying to the Moon (Page 19)

Piano-Four Hands

SECONDO

Flying to the Moon

Two-Pianos, Four Hands

PIANO II

Air <small>(Page 20)</small>
from Haydn's Surprise Symphony

Piano-Four Hands

Air
from Haydn's Surprise Symphony

Two-Pianos, Four Hands

By the Pond (Page 21)

Piano-Four Hands

PRIMO

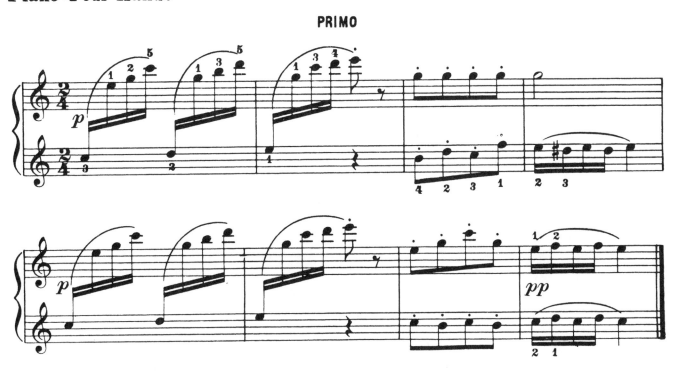

By the Pond

Two-Pianos, Four Hands

PIANO II

Paper Ships (Page 22)

Piano-Four Hands

SECONDO

Paper Ships

Two-Pianos, Four Hands

PIANO II

Sledding (Page 23)

Piano-Four Hands

PRIMO

Sledding

Two-Pianos, Four Hands

PIANO II

The Butterfly (Page 24)

Piano-Four Hands

SECONDO

The Butterfly

Two-Pianos, Four Hands

PIANO II

Questions <small>(Page 25)</small>

Piano-Four Hands

SECONDO

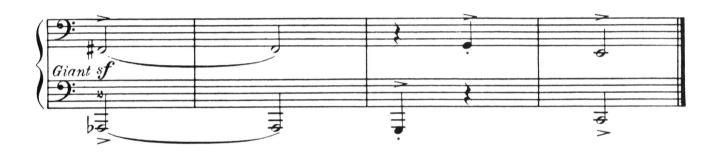

Questions

*Two-Pianos, **Four Hands***

PIANO II

Blue Bells of Scotland (Page 26)

Piano-Four Hands

SECONDO

Blue Bells of Scotland

Two-Pianos, Four Hands

PIANO II

Toy Soldiers (Page 27)

Piano-Four Hands

SECONDO

Toy Soldiers

Two-Pianos, Four Hands

PIANO II

Big Ships (Page 28)

Piano-Four Hands

Big Ships

Two-Pianos, Four Hands

Steam-boat 'round the Bend

Piano-Four Hands

PRIMO

Steam-boat 'round the Bend

Two-Pianos, Four Hands

PIANO II

Comin' 'round the Mountain (Page 30)

Piano-Four Hands

SECONDO

Comin' 'round the Mountain

Two-Pianos, Four Hands

PIANO II

The Long Trail (Page 32)

Piano-Four Hands

PRIMO

The Long Trail

Two-Pianos, Four Hands

PIANO II

The Bee (Page 33)

Piano-Four Hands

SECONDO

The Bee

Two-Pianos, Four Hands

PIANO II

My Bonnie (Page 34)

Piano-Four Hands

PRIMO

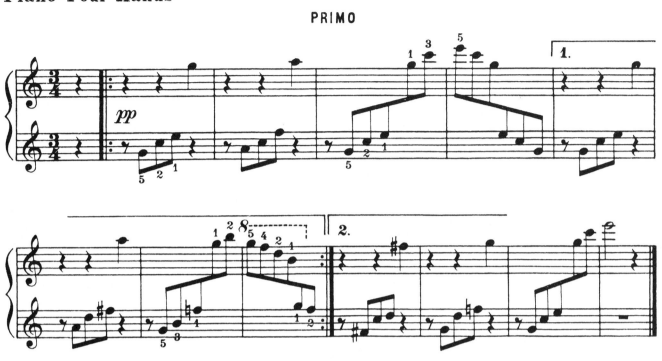

My Bonnie

Two-Pianos, Four Hands

PIANO II

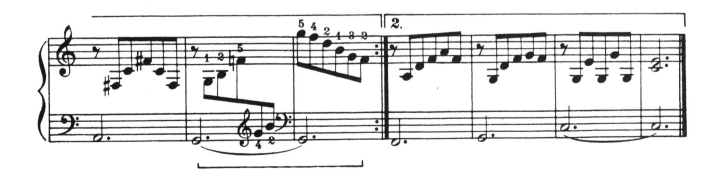

Vacation Time (Page 35)

Piano-Four Hands

SECONDO

Vacation Time

Two-Pianos, Four Hands

PIANO II

Home on the Range (Page 36)

The following arrangement is usable as a second Part either
on Piano-Four Hands or Two-Pianos, Four Hands.

Slowly with much expression

The Juggler (Page 38)

Piano-Four Hands

PRIMO

The Juggler

Two-Pianos, Four Hands

PIANO II

From a Wigwam (Page 39)

Piano - Four Hands

PRIMO

From a Wigwam

Two-Pianos, Four Hands

PIANO II

Biography

JOHN THOMPSON (1889–1963) was born in Williamstown, Pennsylvania, the eldest of four children of James and Emma Thompson. He began music study at the age of five, and his parents encouraged his prodigious talent by sending him to study piano with Maurits Leefson at the Leefson-Hille Conservatory in Philadelphia, graduating in 1909. At the same time, he studied composition with Dr. Hugh Clark at the University of Pennsylvania. In his early twenties Thompson toured the United States and Europe as a concert pianist, receiving respectable reviews and performing with several European orchestras. He was in London when the start of World War I abruptly ended his concert career. After his return to the United States, he began a distinguished career as a pedagogue, heading music conservatories in Indianapolis, Philadelphia, as well as the Kansas City Conservatory of Music (now University of Missouri at Kansas City). It was during these tenures that he developed his distinctive ideas about teaching young children and adults and began his prolific composing and publishing career.

His best-selling method books *Teaching Little Fingers to Play* and *Modern Course for the Piano* were first published by the Willis Music Company in the mid-1930s and soon grew to include the *Easiest Piano Course* and other notable educational publications. These publications have had a profound influence on millions of musicians today, and continue to have an impact on the teaching of piano in America and throughout the world.

NOW AVAILABLE!

CLASSIC PIANO REPERTOIRE
BY JOHN THOMPSON

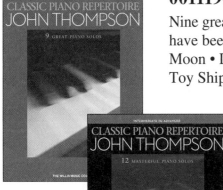

00111968   Elementary (Grade 1-2)

Nine great elementary piano solos by the legendary piano pedagogue John Thompson have been newly engraved and edited for this collection: Captain Kidd • Drowsy Moon • Dutch Dance • Forest Dawn • Humoresque • Southern Shuffle • Tiptoe • Toy Ships • Up in the Air.

00111969   Intermediate to Advanced (Grade 3-5)

Twelve brilliant, evocative and masterful solo pieces by the legendary pianist and composer John Thompson, newly engraved and edited for the modern pianist: Andantino (from Concerto in D Minor) • The Coquette • The Faun • The Juggler • Lagoon • Lofty Peaks • Nocturne • Rhapsody Hongroise • Scherzando in G Major • Tango Carioca • Valse Burlesque • Valse Chromatique.

CLOSER LOOK View sample pages and hear audio excerpts online at **www.halleonard.com**

www.facebook.com/willispianomusic   **www.willispianomusic.com**